MEN AT WORK
by
Bill Witherup

Bill Witherup
March 22, 1991

Ahsahta Press
Boise State University
Boise, Idaho

Acknowledgements:

The Bloomsbury Review "Our President Reads a Book—Not Louis L'Amour"
Contrast (Los Angeles): "At the Cafe Intermezzo, On the Street of Recessive Genes"
Encounter (Kennewick, WA): "Mervyn Clyde Witherup"
Floating Island IV (anthology): "Drake's View Ridge Trail"
"Night Sky: Drake's View Ridge"
"A Rufous: Tomales, 1986"
High Plains Literary Review: "Walking Mt. Vision Trail"
kentucky poetry review: "Common Bill Visits Laird and Lady Randall at Their Country Estate"
Lynx: "Nuke City Ballad"
Marin Review: "Egret: Bolinas Lagoon, 1986"
Nuclear Strategy and the Code of the Warrior (anthology): "To My Father" (revised version: "My Father Dying, 1984")
Poetry Flash: "Variations on an Image by W. C. Williams" (first version)
Swamp Root: "Egret: Bolinas Lagoon, 1986"
Tsunami (Los Angeles): "Hanford: March 1987"
"Doing the Storm Windows"
"Once by Hanford Reach"
"Witherup in Nighttown" (broadside, Lee Engdahl Typography) (revised version: "Mervyn Clyde Witherup")

Editor for Ahsahta Press: Dale K. Boyer

ISBN 0-916272-39-7

Library of Congress Catalog Card Number:
89-80857

Bill of Lading

GRAVEYARD

for Sandra, Mervyn Jr., Constance
and in memory of our father

My father worked for more than thirty years at the Hanford Atomic Engineering Works. He endured an unchanging routine of shiftwork: seven days, seven graveyards, and seven swingshifts. There were two days off between shifts, and an extended three-day weekend at the end of the sequence, called "long change."

I would like to acknowledge James B. Hall's contribution to the book. He read the first draft, then titled **Holocaustics**, and advised a number of structural changes, especially in the ordering of the poems and sections. The title of this collection was also JBH's suggestion. To quote from one of Hall's short stories, say I to him, "Thanks, sport."

Introduction

William Witherup's **Men At Work** is a passionate and carefully detailed memoir concentrating on his public career as a common laborer and his private existence as a poet, friend, thwarted lover, and prodigal son. The poems of **Men at Work** throb with joy, laughter, often pointed at himself, anger, and pain. This book is a testament of thanksgiving to nature, to love, which must include forgiving, and to friendship, as well as a fierce denunciation of the forces that eat away at nature and the bodies and souls of humans.

Son of a working man, William Witherup has been a laborer much of his adult life. In **Men at Work**, he shrewdly depicts the sheer plod of down-and-out-in-the-West tasks: furniture moving, construction, pesticide delivery, desk clerking, truck driving. Thus he has kept body together, save in the many lean periods the post-1973 economy has forced him to face. But, as **Men at Work** reveals, Witherup has dedicated his soul to the hard labor of poetry. As he tells us emphatically in "Charlie Parker, 1989": "Art is labor. Art is rage."

In this collection's first poem, "Root Hog or Die," the laborer Witherup announces, "I can snap a line." He certainly can. Snapping lines out smartly, Witherup rings many changes upon the reader's consciousness: he moves us through tenderly meditative evocations of nature, paeans to friendship, vividly charged sexual encounters, comic and quite political (one of Witherup's strongest concerns is the politics of a wise ecology) analyses of work and the worker's often sub-human position in society, visions of a variety of nuclear holocausts that always lurk in the background, and, finally, extremely touching encounters with death.

Throughout **Men at Work**, William Witherup creates a compelling dramatic tension between the world as it should be or could be, given the marvels of nature and the bonds of friendship, and the world as it is, almost surely dying because of modern man's overwhelming desire for profit and power, which is embodied most fully in his mad, alchemical affair with nuclear energy.

Two carefully crafted poems are keys to comprehending Witherup's heart and his poetic vision. The first, "Sir, If You Are Sir," defines the human's proper labor as "the craft/ Of naming and divining the unnameable flame," the flame of the godhead distributed throughout its creation. A companion poem to "Sir," "A Rufous: Tomales, 1986," features the image of the bird setting the "brush on fire," at which Witherup marvels,

> This
> Is what we were born for.

As in Hopkins. Witherup's things of nature are born to selve, to show forth their own creative fire, and man, too, must follow in the godhead's steps by supplying light, enlightenment, the work of poetry. Instead, as in the final passages of "A Rufous," man responds by fashioning an iron eagle that glows with the fires of nuclear destruction.

At its ultimate core, Witherup's West is a place of beauty. A gifted nature poet, he presents the everyday dramas of nature in "Gathering Blackberries," "Egret," "Drake's View Ridge Trail," and "Night Sky: Drake's View Ridge." For Witherup, delight in the ways of nature as grasped by an experienced and meditative observer is enough, more than enough, for he is "naming and divining the unnameable flame."

In Witherup's visions, men also have their moments of perfection, and they are most finely realized in the poems about friendship: "To Hai," "Walking Mount Vision Trail," "Letter to Byron Spooner," and "Entering the Year of the Snake." Witherup values true friendship highly. It seems to be a declining ideal in a social whirl governed by the growing romance of profit and power.

Witherup also offers us the warm, smoothing grace of laughter, even when his arm has been gashed with a hatchet by a mad Vietnamese major, only because the poor chances of the economy have forced him into undesirable living accommodations and psychic circumstances ("Portrait of S. B. With a Steel Wing"), even when he has been injured on the job ("To Workman's Comp"), even when his fierce sexuality has been thwarted by his poverty and the resulting social circumstance. One of the most wonderful poems in *Men at Work* is a comic myth about the power of woman over the baffled and helpless Satan-Snake ("The Coming of Desire"). In the midst of "Graveyard," the darkest section of the book, Witherup, shifting to prose, delights us with the comic-political tale of his mother's cherry pie, once perceived as a security threat.

Witherup praises and laughs when he can, denounces when he must. Throughout *Men at Work*, the beauty and potential goodness of Witherup's West is threatened by the spread of the manifold poisons of nuclear power:

HANFORD: MARCH 1987

White crocus and purple hyacinth
In the cracked asphalt streets.
Teller-light flickers in the guts
of wild geese preening on the river bank.
Bleached gravels, dead river, white boxcars.

One of the central figures of this collection, Witherup's father, spent most of his adult life laboring at the Hanford Atomic Engineering Works in Washington State and died horribly, a victim of bone-marrow cancer caused by his close contact with nuclear materials. For Witherup, nuclear fire is the fire of evil, eternally opposed to "the unnameable flame," and he creates many frightening visions of its destructive force, especially in "Graveyard."

Men at Work never depicts work in a romantic manner. Witherup makes it clear that many workers are forced to wear Nessus-shirts simply to survive. In "Sir, If You Are Sir" and "Variations on an Image by Williams Carlos Williams," we learn of Witherup's deep sympathy for the plight of workers doomed by contact with poisons.

The final section of the book, "Graveyard," is a true *tour de force*. Witherup sings us close to death, not only in the marvelously compassionate eulogy to his father, "Mervyn Clyde Witherup," but also in the powerful imagistic visions of the deaths of all in the nuclear holocaust, "Doing the Storm Windows" and "Once by Hanford Reach." Along the way, we are asked to sing Witherup's clever "Ballad of the Nuke City Boys," richly basted with black humor. We have been brought dramatically, emotionally closer to the incredible perils of the nuclear fire.

We should be thankful that we have this poet at work on the ground level. Witherup's persona is not the removed, all-knowing, often cynical "I" with whom much of contemporary poetry has made us familiar, but the sensual, passionate I, the what's-really-going-down eye, the I-witness we need, now.

Why hasn't more critical attention been paid to Witherup, Thomas McGrath, and Gary Snyder, the poets truly involved with the actual sweat of work? Aren't these poets, given to iconoclastic social and political visions, the same ones who continually demonstrate their mastery of traditional poetics, a lyrical ear for assonance, alliteration, internal rhyme, and consonance, and a knowledge of stanzaic construction? As **Men at Work** repeatedly demonstrates, "Art is labor," and the best laborers are those who know how "to snap a line." The best message, the memorable one, is always the well-crafted medium.

Robert Schuler
Menomonie, Wisconsin
August 1989

Days

Well, I went to California in the year of Seventy-six,
When I landed there, I was in a turrible fix,
Didn't have no money vittles for to buy
And the only thing for me was to — Root hog or die!

American Folk Song

Root Hog or Die

I'm no craftsman in wood
Or stone masonry.
I'm always the laborer
Or carpenter's helper.

But I've learned this much —
I can snap a line.
A chalk marker, perfectly plucked,
Will leave on stud, sheetrock
Or stone a horizon
Of blue dust.

But today, and last month,
I'm out of work —
There's no call now
For Line-Snappers.

So buddy, or lady,
If you're taking up the trade
Let me give you some advice —
It's — *Root hog or die!*

To Hai
and for George Morf

We thank you, Hai,
George and I,
For your gift
Of red snapper.

You came over
Yesterday morning
Bearing a fish
Stained orange as sunset
And crimson as Vietnam.

Hell, 5,000 lbs
At 38¢ a lb
Is a tough day's work.

Though you won't read
This; can't navigate
The rocky verbs
And strange currents
Of North American English,

You already know,
And have taught us,
Your idea of the word
"Neighbor."

Thanks again, Hai.

To Workman's Comp
for Bill Minor

I

When asked for last words before the noose,
Francois Villon broke wind and said,
"My head will find out now how much my ass weighs."
Hustling-ass myself in the feminine-sounding
Town of Petaluma, I waltzed
Off the walkboard into air, my arms
Full of packing cartons.
It was not as grim as Villon's last day,
But I did find out how much my ass weighed
And the absolute inflexibility of asphalt.
This lumper took his lumps.

II

My problem here is where to end this:
The question of closure in poems written
In free verse and vernacular wit.
If you write in High Court
You come to an end in the rhetoric —
Unless you are one of those scholar-poets
Who never roughened his paws with labor.
Then you might drivel on and on.

III

I still haven't gotten out of this,
Completely loaded the van.
If you wonder why I titled this
To Workman's Comp, it's Economics I-A,
Learned on the job.
After a summer in the meat market
I cashed out on my own beef.
220 lbs of stringy male poet
Paid $640.00 accident insurance.

IV

This manifest then
Comes to you courtesy
Of Transprotection Service Company
Of St. Louis, Missouri
And by way of United Van Lines,
Larkspur, California.
Thus ends my tale
Of how much my tail is worth.

Morning Commute

Freeway is a rope of hornets.
Each of us wants to be first
To get that hunk of dead meat
We call "Our Job."

We would kill, though we
Are socialized, to be No. 1.
But we get by with maiming —
Rolling swiftly on a neighbor
To rip off a wing, a leg.

Let the sonofabitch
Ooze to death — he was going
Too goddamn slow anyway!

Sir, If You Are, Sir

Sir, if you are, sir — the unnameable flame,
Forgive this lapsed Methodist
His present trade: his gear, tackle
And trim; the company truck —
Twelve foot flatbed International
On which he purveys, delivers
Chemical fertilizers; such pesticides
As *Roundup, Ronstar, Surflan, Baygon,*
Metaldehyde, Trimec, Dymec, Gopher Bait,
2,4,D, Mole Blasters — all to blight
And sear the dearest freshness
Deep down things; that a few might golf
On jewelled turf; or Man Suburban
Contemplate a weedless lawn.

Man's smell, man's smudge are everywhere;
The soil is bare and we
Have torn a hole in the very sky.
Nestlings are born blind now —
Yet we can't see the evidence;
Getting and spending we lay waste.

Sir, if you are, sir — your supplicant
Wishes he could work for you daily;
Could walk naked the wild meadows —
Be wafted on flower-light and wind
Up, up, up raptor-like, rapturous.
Yet he is tied down as he ties down
His load, valued for his trucker's hitch —
The craft of ropes; not for the craft
Of naming and divining the unnameable flame.

Variations on an Image by W. C. Williams

I

So much depends
Upon

An orange Clark
Forklift

Crusted with calcium
Nitrate

Beside three tons
Of Turf Supreme

II

Red orange
Mast

Greasy chain
A nearly

Sexual pleasure
Depends upon

Slipping forks
Perfectly into the keys

III

Thrusting steel
Blades

Into the earth's
Guts

So much profit
And power

Depends upon our
Love of *Techne*

IV

So much
Profit

Excessive and
Particular

Profit; forks
Disembowel

Particular countries;
Men with names

V

Particular names
Chevron

Dow, Dupont
Dumping

Unsafe pesticides
On the Guatemalan

Market for instance
So much profit

VI

Depends upon
A laborer

In Honduras
Say

Spraying a fungicide
In the greenhouse

No gloves, no mask
Death his profit

VII

Soldiers in dustmasks
Raise

The dead on
Biers

Fork the pallets
Of body bags

Three tons
of Turf Supreme

VIII

"Take your profit
And shove it!"

My gloves are
Stained

With more than
Nitrates

My Honduran brother's
Scarred, milky corneas

Swings

May works be a test of patriotism as they ought, of right, to be of religion.

Merriwether Lewis, Toast
January 14,1807

Common Bill Visits Laird and Lady Randall At Their Country Estate

Mister Bullfrog had his breakfast
On his chin, a porridge of algae.
He cocked his head at me
And I cocked my head at him —
It was apparent that he,
Mottled in different greens,
Was sitting for an Expressionist.

No, there was no blazing
Blue dragonfly
Astray from a haiku,

But there is an orange carp,
Also in motley,
The palette of Byron's beret.
He sucks and vacuums
The nether carpets and is, like me,
Curator of a sinecure.

At night there is a change
Of tone and wit —
The ghost of Zen Master Suzuki
Strikes the pond's skin
And the moist charcoal sky
Pulses rings and rings.

A Rufous: Tomales, 1986

A Rufous
Mad about the fuschias
Darts and sucks noisily
His soup of nectar and gnats.

I stop shaking
My typewriter castanet
And watch —
His flickering gorget
Has set the brush on fire.

This
Is what we are born for
And from,
A nectar of sperm and flame.

Yet over the Pacific
An *SR 71 Blackbird*
Shatters the air,
Glowing titanium, crimson.

Needle nosed,
Dipping and buzzing,
Its gorget threatens us
With blossoms of nuclear fire.

In Memory of Eve Randall

b. 1924 — d. 1986

When the telephone
Told us she was dying
We had a Sunday kitchen
Full of guests —
But I hurried out
To clean the fish pond.

I raked from the pool bottom
Leaves as black as the ink
On her note from the hospital.
The orange Koi rose to the roiled
Surface, turned and flashed
Back into the depths.

Monday and an empty Guest House
I sat by the cold fireplace
Watching the feathery branches
Of the huge acacia
Brush her name on the November sky.

From a Bed and Breakfast Basement

At ground level
Peonies and white lilac
Think they are clouds.
Holsteins fatten on the April grasses,
Grow rounder and more feminine
Than the Marin Hills.

The old Guest House
Strains at its hawser,
Trying to plunge off to the west,
Into the great waves of crimson light.

All the guests
Have rowed back to town
And to work. They slept late.
They made love;
Promised they would be back.

Below deck the First Mate
Sits on the edge of his bunk
Smoking English Ovals,
Badly wanting a drink.
He and the coffee pot
Are empty, exhausted, chuffed out.

His cabin is damp —
March storms battered the porthole open.
A school of sowbugs poured in.
They wax on the rotting woodwork,
On the flaking paint —
Like Exxon oil executives.

Earwigs, pillbugs, millipedes
Swarm on the First Mate's pillow;
Copulate in his boots.
The cabin blackens with them —
Until the house goes down,

Sucking behind it: cows,
Barns, sheep and a pregnant stray cat
Waiting outside
For a simple bowl of milk.

Gathering Blackberries:
Aug. 6, 1988, Forestville

I wish I could spend three days grieving:
Hiroshima/Nagasaki — fingers purple-stained;
Wrists raw from scratches. How easily
Ripe ones pull off — skin; testicles; nipples —
The largest nearly the size of an eye.
Suddenly we go from blossom to berry to seed.
Dear Christ, Dear Buddha I offer up
One blackberry for each thousand deaths.

Eros on the Russian River

I wake this torrid afternoon
In a landscape of women
But am alone:
A sour man with workman's hands,
Staring at a redwood.

The bark cracks
In the July heat,
Gives way to the passions
Of insect life — boring,
Sawing, chewing;
Copulation in sap.

Guest of stones,
Voyeur to the tree of sex,
I play with the husks of words
While Sunday traffic

Grips the River Road —
Insects driven, swept on,
Tires humming copulation.
Nobody at the wheel.

Our President Reads a Book —
Not Louis L'Amour

Before all the world
Our president kneels on the White House
Lawn; silences his helicopter blades
Alerted to take Ronald Reagan to his wife.

Ronald gestures with his hand
To halt the Secret Service men —
Who are alarmed to see the boss
What? — getting shot, committing *sepuku*?

Now our President takes a book
From his trench coat, reads aloud.
That book is Whitman; it is Rilke;
It is Gabriela Mistral — we are amazed!

As he begins, he chokes up.
He weeps for Nancy Reagan's mastectomy;
Cries for all the women
Under his Administration.

Also, "it seems" children
In Lebanon, Iran, inner Des Moines
Have had legs and arms sliced off
By words from North America.

Then Ronald Reagan stands tall again,
Wipes his nose on his sleeve
And his voice turns over, throbs, hums,
Flattens the grass — lines from Akhmatova,

Neruda beat above us like rotor blades.
We are relieved, we are glad,
Ronald Reagan has become human in public.
We have sought his love for a thousand days.

Charlie Parker, 1989

Art is labor; art is rage.
You think Charlie Parker
Was just some "stoned nigger"
Who went toot-toot? Have you watched
A man hunt? — Charlie could
Outrun any Afrikaaner's whippet.

Our Afrikaaners touch the brims
Of their black hats, say Thee and Thou;
Think they have God's right
To work any "red nigger" to death.

Charlie was in pain. Those black hats
Slice everybody up. Charlie hurt,
But he went to work. He left dust
On their buckle shoes. He ran
That buffalo down — buried his face
In its belly and fed on hot, steaming sound.

Art is hard. You need a tough heart
And good wind. You hyenas, hang back.
Let the lion eat. You'll have your chance
At gobbets. You can whine and fawn then;
Scoot your butts in the dirt.

Long Change

. . . . this writing business as you must know by this time, that it is not as easy to pick up as it looks, a whole lot of them never learn it in their whole life, unless this gift is born in you, it is better to leave it alone . . . . With the limited education I have got at first I shure was up against a hard row of stumps . . . .

Andrew Garcia, Tough Trip Through Paradise

Portrait of S. B. With a Steel Wing

I

Sterling wears now a steel wing,
A pipe organ of struts and screws
Riveting the bones of his left arm.

He's become both Buddha
And wounded falcon,
Has my shaman and falconer.

He rests his arm
On two pillows while we talk.
The irony here

Is that I have come
For therapy about a lesser wound
To *my* right arm.

We enjoy
The humor of the situation —
Both of us savaged

On the plane
Of the Third World:
Sterling by a swerving

Panel truck crammed with *campesinos*;
His client by a berserk
South Vietnamese war lord.

II

On the matter of the hatchet
Attack by Maj. Thong Van Ho,
Sterling says,

"When eating dinner
With a fiend,
Use a long spoon!"

We roar
And belly laugh
Until our arms throb.

My insight for *him*
Is that his arm was nearly sliced off
By a rearview-mirror!

We hoot and whuff again —
(We have a thoroughly
Good time together.)

III

When I leave the hour
Sterling salutes me
With his fractured wing

And I waft out into the air currents
Unhooded, sharper,
Ecstatic in the ultra-violet light.

At The Cafe Intermezzo,
On The Street of Recessive Genes

I am waiting for her, the Asian girl
In the green sweater, the single rope of hair
Over her right shoulder, a single earring hoop
On her right ear.
I am waiting for her to sit on my face
Because I saw her small buttocks
Silhouetted through her dress.

This is a poem about memory,
For the instant you perceive an object,
An idea, a woman
It, she, is already memory.
And already I remember her lovely small nipples
The color of chocolate in my croissant.

This is why sex: this is why intercourse;
This is why fucking never satisfies
Because the moment you are doing it,
Acting it out,
It is already memory.

Her name is Quentin.
I am feeding her a croissant
Under her blue dress
While with her other mouth
She eats a madeline.

She admits she is in love with me —
She saw me across the cafe
Of pseudo-intellectuals.
She knows I'm working class;
She thinks I'm masculine.
She plays with the raspberry nipples
Beneath my red shirt.
She scratches blood from my tattoo.

We were there, at the Fall of Saigon.
We spoke French, we made love.

I write this in words and sentences
Though words are impossible
And syntax lies, even deep syntax,
Like deep sex.

And memory lies. And women lie.
The Viet Cong are at the window.
She signals to them.
She has already betrayed me.

The Coming of Desire

Satan was a mustard eye on a green field.
His hammered scales were rusted
After long duty at the Logos Tree;
His bowels acid with the ration
Of burnished apples; Satan dreamed red meat.

A violet light shone in the rushes.
A smell neither floral nor arboreal
Grabbed Satan's tongue and mustard eye
And just about snapped them out of his skull.
His copper-green tail twitched DANGER.

An animal Satan had not yet seen
Walked out of the reeds. It had
A lion-long mane that flickered
With blue lightnings, like a thunderhead.
Satan radioed, "Logos to Patriarchy!"

Patriarchy sent forth all its power
While centurion Satan laid low,
Jerked with spasms. Adrenalin fanned
Along his scales — He went rigid.
The Logos Tree shuddered; spat fire.

It was a battle of light. The Tree
Crackled silver, vermillion.
Lt. Satan rose to strike, dripping
Mercury, uranium. The animal came on,
Fearlessly: spread its feet in the mud

Until Satan saw a radiance; his tongue
Sensed a heat that was never before
On earth. He knew it was over; he would
Resign his commission; lay his flat head
In that animal's belly; hole up forever.

Egret: Bolinas Lagoon, 1986

Morning. Soap-shaving of a moon.
Sky and lagoon nacreous.
Sr. Ortega y Gasset
Stands reed-still
Examining the muck and weeds
For a metaphysical flash —
The meat of things.

Feathered white snake,
The Beautiful incarnate.
Head poised like a javelin.
Or hunched back on his feathers
Like a scholar
Studying an ancient text.

Even when he stalks
He does not move.
He turns the pages of water
Imperceptibly

While around him
His noisy students, the gulls,
Who have watched
Too much TV
And gobbled excessive junk food
Can't sit still or concentrate.

They thwack and yawp around his desk,
Complaining about heavy assignments.
They do not understand poetry
Or philosophy. They threaten
To tell their parents
And the School Board
That Professor Egret
Is a martinet.

He closes the lesson
With a firm and irritable croak
And slams the door.
His exit is a marginal note
On Aesthetics and the Real.

Disciplined, economic,
Proving less is more,
He gathers the sky and moon
In his monkish sleeves
And makes of his leave-taking
A metaphor.

Chama

Eros and Logos were one to her:
A passion for truth in men.
Her love bites grated on bone.

She left me for love of Nietzsche:
Found men merely mortal;
Went through us all

Like fire in dry chaparral.
An ember smoldered in her womb,
Fed by sexual oils —

Blazed out in the toss
Of her hair. There was
Conflagration everywhere.

Nor am I done with her:
She waits for me
At the top of the stair

Her fevers
Crystallized into the horn
Of 8,000 hungers.

Drake's View Ridge Trail

Flopped down on the trail
In the fragrant pine needles.

Late spring, but already
A hand-span of purpling berries.

A polished black ant
Examines my left forefinger

For some morsel to carry home —
Shall it follow the Left Hand Path?

It is a perfect day —
Violence, war are

Far and distant
Artillery fire.

(The privilege of this pastorale,
having lived to my middle century.)

A hummingbird joins me
In the pine branch above.

She rests, preens,
Thrums her single cello string,

Then flings off to find more nectar —
Play chamber music for another male.

Night Sky: Drake's View Ridge

Spread-winged in my bag
I take the night sky.
The great star clusters
Are fires on a vast plain.

Families gather at each one
To hear grandfathers
Tell stories of the Old Ways.
Grandmothers gum hides
For winter; elk meat is stripped
And drying; huckleberries
Gathered for pemmican.

I sweep closer, perch
In a gnarled oak; watch
A mouse test a pool
Of moonlight.

Then, softly, drums;
Then, softly, chanting
Spreads from fire to fire
Until the entire, vast, deep
Plain resonates with voices,
Ratchets, drums, rattles.

Walking Mt. Vision Trail
for Steve

Walking Mt. Vision Trail
After talking with my buddy —
Who's so full of ambitious desire
He's like a stockyard bull
Hooking cows in the next pen —
I hear typewriter spools
Unwinding between *my* horns.

A black lizard, stamped out
From the unspooling path,
Reminds me, "Pay attention to what's
In front of your snout and boots.
My great ancestors burrowed
Beneath this greasewood root
Before there were such things
As National Parks and poetry prizes."

I pick him up, wanting an English
Word for *Grandfather* other than
A transcription from Amerindian.
"Thank you, Grandfather,"
I tell him anyway,
Turning him belly-up in my palm.

Lizard's orange underside
Matches my sweatshirt, but his eyes
Are a green I don't have
In my palette; then I put him down
Next to a squib of fox shit
Knotted with grass and berries.

Later, back at Steve's
Unfinished cabin, we unroll
And staple tarpaper
Along the studs, joking the while
About *Belles Lettres*
And the poetry hustlings;
Advise each other on the stolid
Yet fidgety emotions of cows.

We are such good compadres
That even grimacing ambition
Is okay between us —
(Once we fist-fought, drunk.)
Path, ribbon, tarpaper —
It takes more than one staple gun
To tack it all down.

Letter to Byron Spooner

Dear Byron: your story
About father Spooner's exit —
"On his last day he asked for music."
And his final request,
"Don't leave my ashes in Tulsa —
I hate this state!"
Though surely it was New Jersey oxides
That took sixty-eight bites from his liver.

I can't help but imagine
Teaspoons over his eyes
Instead of pennies.
(A penny saved is a penny earned.)
The sons get on with it
Carrying urns and puns on the patronymic.

I write this on deathwatch,
My own father withering
In the hot winds of bone marrow cancer —
Yet living as he lived by habit
And will until the blinds are shut,
Clipping coupons to save a penny —
He and mother looking out the window
Upon the Armageddon of the Hanford
Atomic Works — but more concerned
About the junky neighbors.

As you observe
We wait by our fathers for something
Other than advice — a moment,
A flash from the inner life
That will make it all right
For us to weep and grieve.

You and I tagged behind
Our dads on the way to the store,
Turned on the wrong street —
They thought we were lost.
But we are here — we are found,
My father's hand scribbling away
In this hotel room —

Your father beside you
In the booth at the bookstore,
Showing new and classic titles
(Pennies spent, pennies burning);
Passing on illuminated scripts.

Entering the Year of the Snake
Letter to Alan Chong Lau

We write or paint because we are
Seized by images — a cousin,
A Stockton beauty named Millie
In your case; a Kansas City cousin,
Jackie Lou, in mine.

At nine, walking to the store
From the olive-drab trailer camp
In Pasco, in the floury August
Dust, 1944, after a nickel bottle
Of iced cider, I dawdled
At a gravel pit, pushed aside
A tumbleweed and there was
A rattler coiled to strike.
Almost didn't back away —
One nerve flickered *terror,*
But another flashed *beauty.*

Years later that government camp
Is Hanford, ten billion times
More poisonous than any serpent
That dropped out of God's beard.
I'm on my way back from the old
Home town and a gathering
Of the Witherup clan
To honor my dying father.

You and I sit quietly in your
Apartment on Phinney Ave. N.
Sipping mugs of blazing tea —
Kazuko is off to the UW cubicles,
Which you call "her nunnery."
Old friends, we haven't seen each
Other in over a year.
We are suddenly talked out.

It is the image of the two of us
Drinking tea, watching the mottled
Afternoon light on the Boeing Empire,
That stays in my head.
Your New Year's drawing of man
And snake with the witty message,
"Take care of your snake!"
Uncoiled my cold imagination.

The imagination knows that less
Is more. It prefers brief,
Evocative lyrics to prosaic letters.
But the image has been in my notebook
Long enough — I just can't get it
Right, so I belabor it here
And say to you and the world:
Two friends drinking tea in silence
Is an image something like a rattlesnake
Swallowing a meadow lark's egg —
It may feed you for weeks.

Take care of your own snake, Alan,
And your scholar-wife. Watch out
For raptors in 1989, especially
The bald eagle.

Graveyard

I am become Death, the Shatterer of Worlds.
Robert Oppenheimer at Trinity
quoting the Bhavagad-Gita

Now we are all sons of bitches!
Kenneth Bainbridge
Test Director, Trinity

Nuke City Ballad

My home is Rattlesnake Mountain,
I'm bald as a river goose.
Me and my pal, Coyote
Live on wind and yellow cake snoose.

Sing ki-yi yippi
And doo-dah, doo-dah,
I'm a Nuke City Boy!

Oh, we went down to Nuke City
To get drunk and kick some ass,
To grab us a little titty
And piss on the gov'ment grass.

Sing ki-yi yippi
And doo-dah, doo-dah,
I'm a Nuke City Boy!

We bust into Uptown Tavern,
We bellied up to the bar.
When the barmaid refused Coyote,
He showed off his keloid scar.

Sing ki-yi yippi
And doo-dah, doo-dah,
I'm a Nuke City Boy!

Some Hanford boys was there,
They stood us a chain of beers.
They'd never seen such a wonderful scar
In all their forty years.

Sing ki-yi yippi
And doo-dah, doo-dah,
I'm a Nuke City Boy!

Coyote got drunk 'n horny,
Started nipping the barmaid's jeans.
"I don't sleep with dogs," she said,
And radioed in the Marines.

Sing ki-yi yippi
And doo-dah, doo-dah,
I'm a Nuke City Boy!

We had us quite a fracas,
We had us quite a brawl.
We left the Marines and the Hanford boys
A-bleeding, one and all.

Sing ki-yi yippi
And doo-dah, doo-dah,
I'm a Nuke City Boy!

Our home is Rattlesnake Mountain,
Our greens is Russian Thistle.
We get our salt at the Hanford Lick,
And our meat is human gristle.

Sing ki-yi yippi
And doo-dah, doo-dah,
I'm a Nuke City Boy!

Mother Witherup's Top Secret Cherry Pie

I

I have come back to the A-type, government-built, double-decker duplex where I grew up in the Fifties, to visit my ailing father, seventy-seven, who has terminal bone cancer. Merv, as his brothers and friends call him, retired from N-Reactor in 1972, after thirty years at the Hanford Atomic Engineering Works.

Father and I disagree on nuclear matters and foreign policy. And on the virtue of holding a steady job. But I pull my Oedipal punches, in deference to his cancer. It is not for the Prodigal Son to pass judgement — dad's labors in the mills of the National Security State fed, clothed and housed a family of six.

Merv is frail now, down to 135 lbs. But his opinions have kept their weight and vigor. He keeps trying to bait me into a nuclear discussion, much like the hired hand in the Robert Frost poem, who wants one more chance to teach the college boy how to build a load of hay.

When one of the Hospice's nurses stops in to take his blood pressure, pop gets in a dig.

"This is my oldest son, Bill. He grew up here, but he's been trying to shut the place down ever since."

Rictus-like grin, for my part. In the past, when he was healthy, we could never have it out anyway. Rose, my mother, would not allow arguments or heated discussions in her territory. She would shut us off with, "It's time for dinner," or "How about some pie and ice cream?"

Behind every good man there stands a baker of pies, her rolling pin raised like a gavel to rap the house to order.

Here lies the crust of a tale.

II

It is an October afternoon, 1987. A high pressure ridge vaults up all along the west coast, and it is unseasonably warm. Seattle, 200 miles northeast, is talking water rationing. Due west, Mt. St. Helens heats a fresh cauldron of Lava Soup. Some thirty miles northeast of Richland, N-Reactor is on hold and simmer — 11,000 cooks, preps and dishwashers sweat a lay-off. The reactor has been temporarily closed by Public Health: cockroaches were found swimming in the Uranium Soup; rats burrowing in the Plutonium Souffle.

We have just finished an early dinner. Since father's retirement the elders have supped at 4:30 p.m. so they can catch People's Court at 5:00 on the boob. Mother apologizes for serving left-overs, even though her left-overs would put the main course at a classy restaurant to shame.

Merv has gone back to the living room couch, where he holds court now, attired in black Playboy pajamas with red piping. Wasting and bird-boned, he reminds me of a redwing black-bird perched on a cattail.

Here my mother says a variation of her standard line.

"I don't know why I bother cooking — your father doesn't eat enough to keep a bird alive."

Papa Witherup grew up during the Great Depression, one of four children of a grocer in Kansas City, Missouri. After he married mother, he first went to work in a paint store. Following Pearl Harbor, he was hired by Remington Arms, a Dupont subsidiary, in the Quality Control section to check the annealing on cartridges.

When the Manhattan Project kicked into gear, Dupont contracted to build the world's first plutonium reactor at Hanford. Dad was recruited to come west. His first job was, again, in Quality Control. He helped record each graphite block that made up the core of *Ur-Reactor*.

Mama Witherup, nee Nita Rosemond Allen, was the youngest of six children. Her father was a drummer who sold drugstore supplies across Missouri, Kansas and Nebraska.

Rose is one hell of a cook. Her forte was always dessert — especially pie. Her crusts are so light that the wedges levitate on their own and float into your mouth.

Dessert was always the bait and the reward for eating your veggies. Dinner opened with a Blessing and ended with a blessing — provided we four cubs could see our teeth in the cleaned plates.

III

Mother always eats her dessert, with a cup of decafe, directly after the main course, whereas father's habit, after retirement, was to have his pie and ice cream later in the evening.

Though I'm bloated from overeating, I signal weakly that I will join mother over her dessert. My extended visit has given her the excuse to be liberal with the commissary. Food is Love. It is also part of my wages for helping to spit-shine and buff the decks of The Good Ship Witherup — a working class frigate that has patrolled the Columbia River against the assaults of dirt and Communism for almost half a century!

We have our pie at the dining room table while father kibitzes from the sofa. With each visit home I've prodded the old folks to tell me about their childhoods and about the parts of the Richland/Hanford Saga that I wasn't privy to as a youngster.

Neither of my parents are great conversationalists — they are laconic, matter-of-fact, hard-working, Show-Me-Missourians still. But as it is Saturday and there is no People's Court, mother allows herself a bit of free-associating. She tells me about the time, not too long after the move to Richland, when her cherry pie was classified TOP SECRET.

IV

Hanford was one of three highly secret death factories engineered by General Leslie Groves to produce atomic bombs. The other two plants were at Los Alamos, New Mexico (Brain Center) and Oak Ridge, Tennessee (Uranium Milling).

All the engineers and production workers on the assembly line were kept in the political and moral dark about the product of their labors. They only knew that they were performing essential war work.

The workers were not supposed to tell their wives what they were doing at Hanford, or if working women, to discuss it with boyfriends or husbands. Children had even less of an idea. During my nine years of boyhood in Richland, I never knew what it was my father did exactly, as he left each day or swing or grave on *The Grey Goose* on the way to the satanic mills.

Hanford workers and their families, however, were checked and rechecked for political spots or moral stains. Every six months the plain-clothes guys from Military Intelligence would knock on the neighbors' doors and inquire about the Witherups; would rap on our door and discuss the neighbors.

Before the unions were voted in at Hanford, it was hard to make-do for a family of six. My mother cooked up the idea to cater desserts for a little extra grocery money. Her masterwork, the Cadillac of pies, was her cherry pie, with freshly picked Yakima Valley cherries as the nuclear core. She decided to advertise her wares in the local paper, *The Villager*.

V

Shortly after the advertisement appeared, the man from MI sniffed the wind and came knocking on our door. He had seen the advertisement, he said, and had dropped by to sample the product. Rose invited him in — she had a pie cooling in the kitchen. She set out a piece with a cup of coffee; hoped perhaps he was a local businessman.

"My, my," he said. "This is some pie. Sakes alive!"

Then he flashed his Gum-Shoe-Glow-In-The-Dark Badge.

"I'm sorry, Mrs. Witherup, we can't let you advertise your pies. It violates security precautions. But you keep on making these," he said generously, dabbing his mouth with a government issue hanky.

"You can sell these to friends, or by word-of-mouth, but any advertising by Hanford workers or their families is CLASSIFIED. Security, you know — we wouldn't want the Axis to find out what we are up to here, would we?"

VI

It is 4 a.m. I'm asleep in my old room upstairs. I always wake up about this time when I'm visiting, gasping for air like a carp out of water: my folks have converted the original government model to an air-tight, filter-controlled residence. (A Defense System to protect mother's sinuses from dust and nefarious pollens.)

This particular morning I bolt upright, awakened by a pulsing, steady siren.

"Christ!" I think — "N-Reactor has gone critical!"

I throw on a robe and hurry downstairs, open the front door as quietly as I can and listen intently to the radioactive air. Relieved, I decide the siren is merely a car alarm that has triggered, only a few blocks away.

But as I stand there I notice bulky shadows lurking about the re-modeled A, B, C, D, E, and F houses — and I know it is the KGB snuffling window sills for home-baked pies — for there, deep in the sweet juices and sexual hearts of cherry, peach and apple pie lie the State-of-the-Art secrets of the U.S. nuclear weaponry!

My Father Dying: 1984

He burns with prostate cancer.
Carried plutonium home in his underwear,
Ashes of Trinity; Ashes of Nagasaki.

"For Christ's sake, dad,
You went to work daily, out of love
And duty, but did the Devil's job.
You guys stoked Hell's ovens,
Brought home shadows in your lunchboxes.

"All the radiation badges can't monitor
How much your children love you
Or measure thirty years of labor
Smoldering in your work pants;
Or count the sperm spitting across centuries,
Igniting everywhere karmaic fires."

Hanford: March 1987

White crocus and purple hyacinth
In the cracked asphalt street.
Teller-light flickers in the guts
Of wild geese preening on the river bank.
Bleached gravels, dead river, white boxcars.

Doing the Storm Windows

While my birthday turkey
Sweats in the oven
I polish the house's lens
And pray to a God I do not believe
To spare us the flash, the wind, the ice.

Once By Hanford Reach

I cupped an exploded milkweed pod —
The air so still
Seeds would not shake out;
The light in the husk
Both blinding and delicate —
Like that moment at Ground Zero
When eye-pods implode
Dark seeds of death-light.

Mervyn Clyde Witherup
b. July 14, 1910 — d. May 12, 1988

Nearing the end
Father was all bones and pain.
The tumor had eaten him
Down to the rind.

Yet little he complained
Or whined. Sulphate of morphine
Eased him somewhat and he kept
His mind and wit —

Though talking was difficult.
A dry wind off the volcanic desert
Went through each of his rooms
Snuffing out cells;

Left an alkaloid crust
On his tongue. We stood by
With Sponge-On-A-Stick
When he was assaulted by thirst

And images. "Give me your hand,"
He said. "And lead me to
The water cooler. I've been
Up in the sky — I'm very tired."

Then, irritated with us,
He would ask to be left alone.
He'd suck a sponge and grab
The lifting bar; be off again

Brachiating from cloud to cloud.
"Is there a station nearby?
How do we get out of here?
You'll have to help me, son."

He died on graveyard shift.
The train came for him at 3 A.M.,
And when he ran to catch it,
He was out of breath.

Bill Witherup was born in Kansas City, Missouri, on March 24, 1935, the oldest of four children. The family moved west to Richland, Washington, in 1944, where Witherup Sr. found work with the Hanford Engineering Works. A poor student but a "fair high and low hurdles man" in high school, Bill Witherup attended Willamette University, where he ran the quarter mile for the track team. The following year, he attended the University of Washington and "got contaminated by the poetry virus" in Theodore Roethke's class. In 1955, he stayed one week at the University of Iowa, unable to ignore his need for open western spaces. Time in New Mexico was followed by enrollment at the University of Oregon, where he encountered James B. Hall in English and Chandler Beall in Comparative Literature. Instead of taking final exams in the spring of 1957, Bill Witherup joined the Air Force and has been "pretty much on the road ever since."

His publications include books of poetry (**Horsetails**, with Stephen Taugher, Monterey: Peters Gate Press, 1970; **The Sangre de Cristo Mountain Poems**, Northwood Narrows, NH: Lillabulero, 1970; **Love Poems**, Monterey: Peters Gate Press, 1972; **Bixby Creek & Four From Kentucky**, Mt. Carroll, IL: Uzzano, 1978; **Black Ash, Orange Fire: Collected Poems, 1959-1985**, Point Reyes Station, CA: Floating Island, 1986), co-translations (**This Endless Malice: Twenty-five Poems by Enrique Lihn**, with Serge Echeverria, Northwood Narrows, NH: Lillabulero, 1970; **I Go Dreaming Roads: Selections from Antonio Machado**, with Carmen Scholis, Monterey: Peters Gate Press, 1973; **Arctic Poems** by Vicente Huidobro, with Serge Echeverria, Santa Fe: Desert Review, 1974), and a collection co-edited with Joseph Bruchac, **Words from the House of the Dead: Prison Writings from Soledad**, Trumansburg, NY: The Crossings Press, 1975.

Ahsahta Press

POETRY OF THE WEST

Barbara Meyn, *The Abalone Heart*
Cynthia Hogue, *The Woman in Red*
Bill Witherup, *Men at Work*

*Selections from these volumes, read by their authors, are available on *The Ahsahta Cassette Sampler*.